STREAMING TRANSCENDENCE

Copyright@ Bern Kubiak 2016

All rights reserved. No part of this book may be used or reproduced in any manner whatsoever without the written permission from the publisher, except in the case of brief quotations embodied in articles or reviews. Unauthorized reproduction of any part of this work is illegal and is punishable by law.

Library of Congress Cataloging-in-Publication Data

Kubiak, Bern 1968-
Streaming Transcendence/Bern Kubiak
Poems.

ISBN- 13 978-0692663042
ISBN- 10 0692663045

Cover art: Bern Kubiak, *The Madison River,* 2015 Photograph

Printed in the United States of America

MOUNTAIN HIGH PRESS
mountainhighpress@gmail.com

BERN KUBIAK

STREAMING TRANSCENDENCE

NEW POEMS

MOUNTAIN HIGH PRESS

For those who have left us

"WHILE LIVING I WANT TO LIVE WELL"

GERONIMO

Contents

Mid Morning On Granite 3
The Card Player 4
Things You Shouldn't Do 5
Bacon And Eggs 6
Another Illusion 7
Travelers 8
The End Of The Bar On A Friday Afternoon 9
Sun 10
Ah River 11
The Road I 12
The Road II 13
The Road III 14
The Road IV 15
The Road V 16
The Road VI 17
Farm Girl 18
My Faith 19
The Last Trout 20
Howling 21
The Eyes Have Spoken 22
Walking Winter's Dialogue 23
Blue Light Special 24
Beds 25
Christmas Pierogies 26
January 27
Water 28
Lake Fishing With Mother 29
And Here I Am 31

Blood Moon *32*
Trout Dog *33*
The Bear In Us *34*
Ritual *35*
Bag Of Tricks *36*
Cardinal *37*
Seattle Peep Show *38*
Gaining Speed *39*
Zodiac *40*
Grade School *41*
Fish Fry *42*
Early Morning *43*
Spring Flowers *44*
October On A Hillside Along The Dunraven Pass *45*
Brains *46*
Birth *47*
Poor Kids *48*
Clarity *49*
Easter Beard *50*
Searching For A Muse *51*
In The Name Of The Father *52*
Hop Yard Harvest *53*
Streaming Transcendence *54*

STREAMING TRANSCENDENCE

Mid Morning On Granite

I climbed to the top of the mountain.
I looked and saw no one below.
In the clouds that were slowly engulfing me,
a haiku was drifting along.

It read:

The sage is not here-
please sit on a rock and take a number,
help will soon arrive.

The Card Player

She is up before dawn playing solitaire as the coffee drips in reverse, slowing down the rise of the impending sun. Shades are drawn low, permitting a sliver from the outside to the inside. A twenty-five hour day only happens in scripted movies with all-star casts. We all want a little extra time sent our way, but the keeper is always dismantling our efforts to do so with an abundance of modern day endings. It doesn't appear to bother her, as there are things to do. The calender days have been good to you mother. The sound of cards clicking are like cicadas on a summer evening. Both rhythmic to the ear, as their impending cadences are stop and go, just like the days that surround us. We all have a hand to play. The shuffle of her hand was dealt over seventy-years ago. She knew more of the game than most. Her relaxation is played out all over the kitchen table, as we are children playing in adult costumes. Nobody really sleeps past sixty-five. One eye is open as to make sure the earth doesn't swallow us whole. Your features warm as you meet the light at the edge of the porch. Pausing and holding, you set the tone of the day. You gaze towards the pine-laded hillside and aged sepia-toned fence, and welcome life's subtle encroachment.

Things You Shouldn't Do

Create robots for sex. Bother the aliens. Shoot elephants. Drive with your pants off. Keep beautiful brooke trout. Eat food out of cardboard boxes. Bet on horses. Enslave the poets. Wear name tags to work. Drink cheap beer. Take pictures with a flash. Listen to drunks with a political agenda. Tuck your shirt in. Not travel. Invade other countries. Sleep at interstate road stops at three in the morning. Watch reality TV. Give up. Get tattoos of dead relatives. Put ice cubes in expensive single-malts. Slide head first. Attend Christmas Mass drunk. Gossip. Take road trips with ex-lovers. Shave delicate body parts. Touch animals at National Parks. Ski backwards. Go to tent revivals. Climb wet rock. Wear three piece suits. Travel by bus. Eat other people's space brownies. Attend faux country concerts. Inhale second hand smoke. Hang the Confederate flag. Take kids to the Vegas strip. Swim with sharks. Vote for people wearing too much hair product. Lie to custom agents or your mother. Retire to Florida. Name your kids after a fruit. Catch a garter belt with your teeth. Dance the chicken dance sober. Try on-line dating. Alter the survival of nature. Join a mega church. Marry a stripper named Xanadu. Swing at the first pitch. Wear cotton in winter. Speak with a fake accent. Fish with live worms out of a can. Proselytize in my hood. Wear pirate earings when your not a pirate. Plan an expensive wedding. Vote for a person who quotes the Bible a bit too often.

Bacon And Eggs

The sun broke through the shutters this morning at seven. The cock crowed but it was only in my dream. I can hear the coffee pot breathing its breaths. I lay there motionless, but who is in the kitchen? I am alone underneath these flannel sheets. No sexy, soft maiden to speak of this morning. Mother is watching the grandkids, and dad left ten years ago. The day he died, he was up at three in the morning looking at family photographs. What did he know that November morning? He told me nothing of course. I can hear the neighbor shoveling the ice and snow that came down last night. The metal against cement is grating me and forcing me to rise. I spent the previous night in the public house speaking to beer wenches who love their winter ales and men who will buy them. Looking into the mirror, I now have new character lines that run east to west, and my eyes are dark around the edges. Halloween has come and gone, but what character am I playing today? I now remember I set the coffee pot on timer, but no noise coming from the cast iron skillet. What is this cruel joke I'm wondering? I am in my old boyhood room. I can see the crucifix on the wall. Jesus is the same. The blood has lost its color. The few trophies that I won, are long gone as my eye sight is ever so blurred. The thin shutters are allowing me to squint through the window into the morning of optimism. I want to hear Sunday mornings polkas and smell grease fat with bacon and eggs. But the only gods I know have long passed to the other side.

Another Illusion

The poem presented itself to me in a dream.
She told me that I would need to make love to her
in a haiku form. "Traditional, I ask?" She said, "Is there
any other way?" I took her P off. I moved to her O and E.
M was waiting still. As the letters were spread across
the room, she realized that certain historical literary
rules should not be applied to our eastern lovemaking
principles. I tried not to spell. Her words were worlds
away from me that I knew right away. Five, seven, five,
were thrown out of the window. They floated in the air
before landing in tiny paper boats, that drifted down the
street after the rainfall. We were finally free of academia
now, as a rush of our own nakedness grew out of hunger.
We were right. It only mattered to us.

Travelers

A lone seagull seen along the three rivers. In flight, remnants of a childhood glider. Frozen northern wasteland of the great lake brings you south against these city-spaces of Penn's woods. I am befuddled as you perch alone atop of a garbage can. Naked against the wind, you twitch your little neck like an addict needing a score. I burn aged maple as the locomotive wind creeps down the flue. Lurking shadows from the embers of back light, move like prehistoric hand puppets. Your swirling is dizzy unlike Gillespie, as you say nothing. I move only to feel the heat and to melt the slowness away. I am just a winter scavenger like you. We both are drifting in the air below the sub arctic surface, looking for bits and pieces of a puzzle that seems to have been taken away months ago by that bitch mother nature.

The End Of The Bar On A Friday Afternoon

Grasping through the thickness of humid air, I see past the short-shorts you wear this late Friday afternoon. Flanneled shirts outweigh the suits and ties as their grunting and laughing set the tone. You entertain the drunken bar men and their misogynistic smiles. You will graciously listen for the extra change. They paw at you without claws, and tip hefty to sneak a gaze at your tramp stamp butterfly, which flutters when you bend over. You are the lioness who is caged behind the bar. You look hungry to check out the meat in front of you and take the many drink offers. Echoing acoustic swills from a distant time, you move to play the single-play jukebox. The yeoman types speak of Bunyan-esque stories of their week at work. No flashy ten dollar drinks. They appear to own the red leather top swivel bar stools their bodies occupy. Their narrative is drunk loud but not drunk obnoxious as they chat to their new best friend sitting next to them. They don't speak of the stock market or cry about monies lost. They pay cash for their drinks. Is there such a thing as "happy hour?" For the other twenty three hours, life is just a dollar more expensive. And when the hand hits six, the next crowd wearing the better shoes, arrive to begin their own working narrative after their eight hour shift of life ends and a new one begins.

Sun

The sun died last week and was replaced with nothing.
Silence followed with the undertones of dull colorless matter,
that filled the clouds with clown tears, madness, and extra
gun clips. This sent people mad to kill in office buildings,
grocery stores, and movie theaters. The gun lobby paraded
down K Street, and threw candy, shaped as machine guns
to grade school children. The nation wept for ten minutes
after the last mass shooting occurred. We all forgot about
who died when our favorite show came on about nothing.
I stayed indoors and wrote a long love letter on yellow paper
with separated lines of light blue. My cursor was as imperfect
as our species is in black and white. I sent my letter to a girl
who sips agave on her front porch. She listens to the music
of the rattlers and hummingbirds. My hopeful words perhaps
will find her along the great San Juan and float down stream.
And maybe after reading it, she can find me a new sun,
against the cloudless sky and send it back my way.

Ah River

Coming to you, I see white masses. You're covered with
numbing after thoughts. A trickle, of free flow winding
down from the highlands from deep beneath the core,
is fluid symmetry. Iridescent, spotted creatures, created
when no one was looking, idle in you. Broken limbs,
disemboweled trunks, the mossy green lichen dripping
like old paint remain attached. Motionless in the slow drift,
I watch eons pass over my boots, as I'm tip-toeing on borrowed
time. Haggling for time doesn't seem like a bad idea today.
Crunch, crunch, yesterday's flakes formed this forgotten
landscape of a winter shell that will remain impassable for
months. Why I come back to you, only leaves me with a
beautiful misery of release during this time. No shade is needed
from the eastern hemlock at the cutbank, as grey will remain
until the days grow longer. No movement in that water you
see; gin colored with misshaped rocks reflecting of another
year of passing. I recognize myself as the nimble jester, who
listens to his own jokes while navigating an afternoon of
trickery and youthful Tom Sawyer-ing. I crossed you a number
of times. I sense you will continue and another season will
welcome you, but will I?

The Road I

I look at her with determination. My Chevy is packed
with my life once again. 1850 miles. She has never
failed me. The morning is early. Crisp. Dark. A fluttering
of white is the sky. I see the beginning of time start again
as soft light welcomes the orange geometric shape that
is rising behind the granite in the distance. Like a balloon,
it nearly sits atop the highest peak, ready to pop, and deliever
us eternal light. It is Sunday in Utah. The gentile is on the road.
I tithe for caffeine from this woman behind the counter. An
indigenous beauty. She is a raven, with eyes and hair of black.
I am a pioneer drifter from the east. She speaks little, but
wishes me well. The endless cement awaits me in my cosmic
trance, that will take me far past a million steps of buzzing
metal chariots. My tank is full. It is April and tired old snow
still covers the brown hills of dense scrub oak and wild grasses.
I look out the back window and bird woman is behind me,
disappearing with each mile until she is gone like my espresso.
It has kicked me towards the haunting landscape of western
Wyoming.

The Road II

I-80. Roads glazed with the transparency of rice paper. The blowing of wind against the sage loaded landscape, makes me think of the 1840's when handcarts were being pushed across night and day by the faithful. I desire neither multiple women nor salvation. The sky has no boundaries, nor does the time I will spend buying and burning gas for the next few days alone in my spaceship of four wheels. Flying J outside of Rawlins, Wyoming, selling gas at $3.25 for eighty-five. It is the usual suspects pumping gas at five degrees. Truckers are warriors loading up their diesel, cigarettes and beef jerky. The snow has begun once again coming in from the north, spreading sugary treats, as I am roughly three hundred miles into this nonsense. I am dreaming of that final push along the river of that near deserted industrial town. Only fifteen hundred to go.
The illusion of madness and the reality is that I am not a Kerouvacian character. I am writing my own road novella. I force myself to grab the wheel, take a swig, and make one final look at the neon cowboys, and their frozen, horse shit-covered trailers and head for Nebraska. Big Red. Sand Hills. Corn. I see pioneer children suffering along the rutted-wheel landscape. Following leaders can even make yoga girls get the blues. Don't quote the verses, as I am not waiting for rewrites anytime soon.

The Road III

The "Corn Husker State." Yet another corpse of a deer welcomes me to the state of Nebraska. I was hoping for a Kooser poem at the rest stop. This is where the road begins to take hold of you. It grabs your hands as you gaze from left to right, fighting the flat light of roadside barrenness. The harvest has passed months before. All the guts of these states and towns, are just a few miles off the endless exit ramps tempting me to explore. Pushing at seventy-five with the sun and wind behind me, creates an even flow of rhythmic stillness of post orgasmic satisfaction. I don't smoke. I predate nothing here. Gothenburg has their pony express and sod house museum. It's closed today. A historical plaque that has collected the dust of a past, tells of a rich Swedish history. Three thousand, five hundred and seventy four people call this old rail town home. I move slowly in town with out of town plates. I see blue lights, but not for me. The sidewalks are cleaner than the air itself. A near empty diner with bits of their neon sign working just above the door, reads "FOOD." Advertisements of a working man's meal light up the glass front. New migrant workers in white cowboy hats, checkered shirts, idle around vintage pickup trucks pressed against main street America. I manage to follow the old granary to the interstate once again. You are so long Nebraska. There should be two of you.

The Road IV

The road is filled with stories of excitement, danger, loss, and serrated segments of our own thoughts of being somewhere else. Up early with the smell of a mid-range hotel breakfast buffet, I hear sounds of doors opening and closing, with families laughing. There is chatter in the hallways from worker bees getting ready for another day of cleaning, often invisible to most people. I drink the coffee that is offered in styrofoam. I have been here before. Different cup and same swill disguising as road coffee. Some people never learn. My truck is just a protective membrane that I want to shed soon and walk among the trees and tall grass that will hide me from the masses. The smell of spring has taken on buds in the Midwest. Nothing like burning diesel and cow shit. I will soon maneuver across the prairie trying to catch the morning, moving sun that can't help itself with its own omnipresence of warmth and guidance. I see the yellow static lines that have kept me from wavering into another consciousness and other people's lives. I switch the dial from evangelical radio hacks, to Young singing about "Cowgirls in the Sand." I'll take the later and keep my eyes for leather chaps and Malibu tans, even though I am going in the wrong direction.

The Road V

As I have now driven over the great river, I have arrived in Twain's Hannibal. The lights of the bridge flicker and the moon permits me to see the Mississippi below the girders of steel. The raft and the boy Finn shared the same night sky, as I remembered reading as a teenager. The rain has finally come again, as dime droplets become quarters in mere seconds. The movement of the wipers are as hypnotic and as repetitious as a low grade magician at a state fair. There is no stopping tonight, as the roll of thunder is present, and the sky is delivering. The rolling hills of eastern Missouri are showing me their state motto. With darkness, the state sponsored rest stops are my temporary home. I see the night ghosts appear with mop and bucket in hand. They roam the shadows of dimly lit deposit stations. The heavy smell of Lysol is better than espresso. I see the map on the wall that tells me where I am and where I need to go. No smart phone needed here. Big trucks with lights hum in the parking lot as I cover myself up with sleeping bag to drone out the nearby interstate traffic. The rain stops as I wake hours later to a clearing, morning sky. I think I am in Indiana. Ain't that America, and I don't see any more pink houses for you or me. I am now getting a different type of flat that stretches into Ohio, as borders mix like cheap drinks at a fire hall wedding.

The Road VI

The eastern flank of America has its flat cities and giant roman-inspired sports stadiums that sparkle in twilight against all their glass. I listened to Guthrie on public radio this evening. It is my land and yours. Take yourself out to it. I have five hundred miles with you. How many more times will I make this trip? The drivers are getting worse with their self-obsession of not driving, but mimicking the art of paying attention. To die in a piece of wrapped steel makes me shudder. I want to walk among the beasts and fuel my heart with blood. Passing cows with disinterested smiles makes me hungry. There are hundreds of you who will be served in yet another road-side attraction. The rather homogenized interstate travel is packaged like these happy meals in red and yellow.
 We travel fast, we eat fast, and we tend to screw fast. We all need to regain consciousness. I blinked past Indianapolis and Columbus and the final push is very near. I will consume packaged meats and heart pounding elixirs. There are river bends and steep death grades which burn brakes and rigs.
I am tired. Like a trout in the riffles, I am dodging the five o'clock shuffle. People just want to be home, like me. I race from left lane to right lane. I speed. I stop. I roll down the window, and smell my past and present. I become once again familiar not with faces but with places. I know this road. I travel through the yellow brick tunnel. I smell the river that runs next to the road. I see the barges of coal. I feel the old rust of a city with a new skyline. I climb that final hill. I pull up that driveway. The door opens. Stick it Thomas Wolfe. Sometimes you can go home again.

Farm Girl

Underneath the girl's dress of daisies were panties of cerulean blue. The corn in the distance was nearly eight feet high and soon to be picked. He was not slightly interested in the sweetness of that yield. The dogs barked, greeted, and soon sniffed him. He stroked both of their heads gently and put them at ease. They seemed satisfied, but stayed near their mama, the human. I suppose she choose him that evening. They laid below the highest tree that they could find, and let the wild grasses comfort their tanned bodies, that were darkened by the month of July. He did not resist such a offering of watermelon, her youth and his willingness just to say yes. The smell of tomatoes were but a few feet away; red, round, and hiding beneath the greenery of vegetable shyness. They soon forgot what they both had left to be here in the moment. Her strong hands from field work were rough, but yet desirable to the touch. Their wishes were reaffirmed through the silence and totemistic impulses. Smells of robust body musk and circus moves were introduced, while a bluegrass banjo strummed by a mountain garage band somewhere down the dirt road, as day became night on the farm.

My Faith

The harvest. Homemade beer. A cold river. Funny women. Greek cured olives. Morning sun coming through a window. Native trout. Neon bar signs. Country markets. Hidden cabins in the woods. Open skies. New snow. Family. High desert silence. Sleeping outside. Solar systems. Pizza with red wine. Dresses with floral prints. Long drives with the windows down. Camp fires. Wild animals in the back woods. Fourth of July. Hooting barn owls on a summer evening. Love making that doesn't require a diamond ring. Brothers who won't screw you over. Mothers who never judge. Fathers who were involved. Preachers who help the indigent. Bright colored leaves on old country roads. Carrot cake on birthdays. Gardens that grow garlic and hops. Late summer fly hatches. Endless laughter. Roads that take you away and sometimes don't bring you back. Old churches. Stories from grandparents. Children playing baseball. Frozen custard. Rock and roll. Old poets who live on with their words. Random kindness. Your first childhood friend. Palm trees that move with the impending, evening storms. A green flash over the sea at sunset.

The Last Trout

If you were the last trout would I try to catch you?
The osprey that flies above would certainly take you
to the nest. Half way between the darkened line of
endless ridges and encroaching days end, your alien
body approaches the surface. The muddied, overgrown
riparian willows and towering cottonwoods is your hole
in the wall hide-out. You find the last of the golden stone
flies and take them into your belly one at a time. I see a
glimpse of haloed spots that break within the rush of the
moving tail-water. White foam bubbles up and against
the well packed rocks, as you move deep along these fine
edges searching for more food and coverage. Spooking is
easy; as my shadow has etched itself into these waters in
giant proportions. I witness a deafening leap, a time lapse
splash near the barely hidden rocks, where I think the last
trout may go. I will follow the light until there is no more,
and try again tomorrow.

Howling

When the night air is so cold, time and space are simply trapped in a jar, that we open up during the thaw. A lone buck paid no attention to my alpha vocals, and kept foraging for winter edibles. My voice found its way through the cluster of hardwoods and narrow valleys. From cemented cities and rural landscapes, I am now back in a youthful place of rusted playgrounds and frozen ball fields. Returning to these fields on imaginary fours allows the nape of my neck to feel the chill of single digits, and the survival of my past. My belly is full of meat and vegetables. I am a wolf on a clear night. I take the self induced, primal tunnel and look to see what happens next.

The Eyes Have Spoken

His last worlds have been spent between a heaven for
dogs and the purgatory of man. He has come to us.
I wonder what he dreams as he sleeps all afternoon?
Does he run through the endless fields of his youth
and have any remembrance of time? He only speaks
with his eyes. He eats his hard boiled eggs and he looks
to me for a pat on the head. I can see a thousand
years of time as I look into his stare. Where does my
four legged friend get to go after all this suffering?
Time is film grainy, as the road comes to a close at the
horizon. Your ailing will be no more. There will be no
judgement. We are always shedding layers until there
isn't anymore to wear.

Walking Winter's Dialogue

A wintry maze lays in front of me. My thirst has grown heavy as my mind wanders like an old drift boat in a storm. Here at the edge of the unknown path of January's cruel passage to middle age, is a sudden stillness like that of an open prairie, dark alley, or high mountain pass, as in nothing is moving. We think time slows because of this hibernating period; trickery of the mind by the body. I find solace beyond the silent echos of the multiple worlds that surround me. There is no hooded monk in a ghost tree whispering me instructions on the future. I'll find my way back, and sit against the stone wall, and wait for the fire to warm my ticking heart to move forward.

Blue Light Special

I am waiting in line to return something I didn't need the day before. My plastic bag has hair color of medium brown. I decide to say no this time around. Healthy gray on the sides will do. I wonder if she will internally make judgment? A goddess working at Kmart in a small town. Tucked behind a customer service desk, she waits for the next returnable item that always has a story to be told. Mine is simply that I want the color of my youth. The returns have piled up like an overused land fill. The way she is moving the price-checker over the twenty cans of cat food, that the heavy-set man has placed before her, is putting me in a trance. Like a female Copperfield, she has gained my attention. Does he not know that this counter is for returns only? He must have seen you from afar, like myself. Your blond hair, like braided rope, lays over your broad shoulders. Bright, cherry lipstick that was probably bought in aisle four, is perfect, painted on your lips. Your pleasantness is due noted. Will management be in your future or the cover of some magazine? The bearded cat lover took his time to make small talk in between food for his feline and tiny sausage snacks he purchased for himself. The cold February air continued to push through the automatic doors as shoppers moved with diligence towards blue-light specials. As I anticipate my turn, it appears that Mary, her co-worker calls me over to exchange my item. She looks at me with all her weight and homeliness and says, "Honey, you don't need any hair color." She either has something in her eye or she is winking at me.

Beds

Hard, soft

wide, large

rustic, urban

I slept in many

kept, unkept

hot and cold

for reading

and screwing

naked in the winter

clothed in the summer

I think it's time to sleep

on the floor with the rest

of the animals.

Christmas Pierogies

Flour, water, salt, butter, yeast, potatoes, farmers cheese and onions. Shots of vodka. Clear as high country streams and without communist influences. I drink like a dock worker from Gdansk. Tree lights in the distance, glowing like colored, distant stars. I see them from the kitchen window. With perfect unison and arrangement, it is the teller of time. Blue spruce, ten bucks from a bearded monk-pagan, who let me borrow his only saw. Pierogi making began in a crowded wood frame house on Linden Avenue. Immigrants living in a flood plan. Pollacks. They made it their own. I'm no babushka mama, but this is natural to my hands. Sweat drips, slipping away from my brow onto the floor and mixing bowl. Geometric shapes taken from the bottom of pint glasses. Stretch the dough, wet the dough, flour the dough, insert the rolled ball of potato. Immersed into the waters below. My boiling font is to nourish and cleanse. Repeat. The kitchen smells of pan fried butter and raw onions. My eyes weep. I do think of them. These smells and traditions is what I have left of them. Another year of dough-caked hands. Four dozen should be enough. I lose track of the shapes and sizes that resemble the winter mess. Four minutes later and they are ready to eat. The snow and wind continues to shape the exterior, as I finally sit in flour and sweat. Indulging in a boyhood pleasure of pocket filled shaped staples from the old country, brings me no greater joy on this December evening.

January

Frozen earth is silent, but yet I can feel vibrations
underneath the layers of our own history together.

I already know that you left this grand party a
decade ago. No cake nor candle. No stories from the past.

Perhaps a review in pictures and a late night toast of
Canadian grains that you left for your boys to drink
will occur in your honor.

I am not fooled by time any longer.

As I walk between the worlds, nothing appears to
slow down enough to hear your thoughts.

Winter wind breaks the branches that hold specks of
snow. After life theories will disappear into the air that
I steal from the dream world.

Stars that are placed in the moving sky like chess pieces,
choose not to move. Our galaxies don't ever answer
each other. Maybe it takes a million years to break the
silence or maybe I am not trying hard enough?

No omens to take notice, as I lean against the bark of
an old tree. Where are you old man on this January night?

Water

Bluebird day fills my olfactories with pinyon pine. Sounds of depth and roar that symphonies could not match bring me closer. Your blue mass twists against the bends and moves from the distance of my eyes that match you in clarity and color. Edges of desert soil speak of clear lines and sharp turns. April shows itself with only days away with musical rebirth. Chasing the western sun, and breaking in and disappearing between cuts in the earth, I can hear the sounds of vipers chanting from the sage surrounding me. Sandstone walls shoot up like ancient cities in an oasis. It is easy to seduce me with what follows. If I don't return this time, it's because I have joined them in another world of flowing water and gilled bodies.

Lake Fishing With Mother

Opening day 1978. Trout in suburban America. We dug our worms the night before with the night light, that shimmered against the damp wet grass of the backyard. Soil like an Irish bog, blackened our fingernails. We used gardening tools that mother used for flowers, and rusted pails with tiny holes for our sacrificial worms. Dad wasn't much of a fisherman, but was the supplier of our rod and tackle. He sported a Pall Mall cigarette between his meaty fingers, and a whiskey manhattan in his grip after another day at the grind. He watched us for a good hour. Then he told us how the nearby industrialized river nearly killed him a few times while swimming there when he was our age. "Don't go anywhere near the Allegheny." Mother nodded in accordance. We also knew the story of the two young boys who walked on the ice that same year and who were never seen again. Footprints on the early March ice and nothing else. The river got them and we knew it. We weren't looking for monster catfish or bass in the river, we wanted to go trout fishing. Mother was in charge that morning. The eggs were runny and sunny with specs of pepper. The toast; buttered, slightly burnt and dipped in ketchup. It was like Christmas morning. Dad worked overtime growing up, but he would be back in time for fish dinner. I can see the look on mother's face as she hoped we would catch and release the stocked rainbows before lunch.

Although thirty years have passed, I still remember well that morning of the second week in April, the month of the resurrection, pirate baseball, and rainy days. It had all been overshadowed by the trip to a local lake, where too many kids and their fathers had gathered. The three kids from Fairmont Drive had wanted to be the first ones there as we piled out of our brown Chevy station wagon, with Zebco reels in hand. We all had fat night crawlers hanging on those Eagle Claw hooks ready to be dunked. Children were lined up like a cheap buffet around the edges of the lake. This was not a good sign. The lake was carved by ancient backhoes before we were all born. The posted signs were everywhere. Fishing begins at nine. We all joked that the fish had to get ready as well. Don't take the first worm you see. Stay away from artificial lures. Maybe they didn't stock this lake we wondered. Could all the hard work the night before be worthless? We even went to bed extra early and missed our Friday night shows. Billy was seven and liked the idea of fishing, but would rather have skipped stones that morning. He ate all his snacks before ten. Brian found a spot near the high grass, hiding himself from the waters below. He told me that he read it in a book to hide while fishing. So I decided to sit next to mother on a bench and cast from there. The red and white bobber soon took a plunge like an accused witch. "Bernie," my mother chimed. After what felt like a huge struggle, the fish emerged from the algae infested water. It wasn't a trout after all. To my dismay, a rather medium size bluegill. And that morning, there were many bluegills caught on the gobs of worms we had handpicked the night before. It didn't matter. Dad was waiting for us. The great fishermen had returned. He made a dinner of steak and potatoes. No fish. Mother took us a few times after that.

And Here I Am

I have breached the front door, and did what I wanted
many times over. Nearly a half-century of creating my
own narrative, I re-read the chapters once more. The kid
who played. The adolescent who questioned. The adult
who listened. The man who beckons for a little more.
Dreams have come and gone, like the people who once
stood next to me. Invisible energies are spoken like history.
We are rewarded by what they left. The day has become
night, and light flickers like the cosmos from the space above
me. And here I am to see if a new story is in the making.
I make room on the shelf for those stories to come, and throw
away the calender that sits above my desk as I can't bear
thinking of the silent clock that is ticking away.

Blood Moon

Is it the end of the world as we know it? I sit on the
porch and stare far past the darkened edges of the sky.
I see transparent faces riding the falling stars. Distant
in miles, their hearts beat back against the walls of the
solar system. Blood moon. You came and went. Some
of your evangelical followers prepared for the four
horsemen. No need for duck tape and tin rations, as
this is it. Their salivating madness of scripture is impressive;
and the sun became black as sackcloth of hair, and the
moon became blood. The world has always been mad
since cave dwellers tried to saddle up a T-Rex and ride
them up to the nearest swamp pit. I'd rather just eat the
snack mix and offer it up to God who controls the on
and off switch.

Trout Dog

He heard me coming through the thicket of ferns and aged oaks. The creek had the color and movement of his chocolate coat filled with burrs. He was the brown current that was everywhere I stepped. He appeared at the waters edge to greet me like an old friend, and decided not to leave me that Sunday afternoon. He was the "trout dog." I casted, he jumped. I mended my line, he barked. I waded into deep holes, while he navigated the current towards me. I paused to change flies, he quizzed me. He was communicating with the trout below, I assumed. He was the guardian of spring fed creeks. Although he welcomed me, he became the merry prankster. I could not lose him in between the thorn thickets and rusted railroads tracks. He was the ghost dog of the backwoods. He spoke the language of the woody woods. The trails new him. He ran hard up and down the endless bends of the darkened forest. As the day grew longer, I surrendered. The sky formed clouds with mash potato intent. The wind began to thrust the trees in wild unison, all while the "trout dog" walked me to my truck. I mumbled to him of lost gear and no trout, but he provided no sympathy and soon took back to the woods.

The Bear In Us

I just pitched my tent in a circled arena of ponderosa pines, elevated just beneath the cathedral like spires. There is no noise; but my imagination thinks otherwise. Vibrations in the still makes this raw. I had seen my first bear at the Pittsburgh Zoo. The exhibit was built during the grand public works of the 1930's. The bears were ratted up looking, stuffed animals portraying what they never got to be. I would stare at them with my brothers. We were able to toss peanuts from a dispenser for a quarter. They didn't care. That was what they knew. Without wildness, apathy takes over. Aren't we all sometimes trapped in being something else? I am an extension of the landscape this evening. I make a fire that burns until darkness has taken over. My heart beats a bit faster with every encroaching sound. I will be certain that I am not living in a three dimensional diorama. We all have that bear in us.

Ritual

He searches for the paring knife, wood handle, cheap blade. He finds the grandest apple he can find. The steel shank slowly cuts, releasing the smell, grown in his backyard orchard. The porch has his favorite chair. White, plastic, and high back. After bracing against the rusted railing, he sits in the corner on top of the orange colored tile he placed there fifty years prior, under his feet. He cannot bend like a sage, but he can elevate himself above street level as a rounded Buddha grandfather. In the awakening light of dawn, he will listen to the birds and the still of the neighborhood. The juice of the apple will drip and hang on his weathered hands. He will consume slow and deliberate, as if he is taking in the divine. Kitchen lights from across the street will begin to look like small fires glowing from ancient caves. Morning shadows will again move back and forth, rustling the inhabitants that the old man is happy to see. He knows that he has awakened from the dead dream once again.

Bag Of Tricks

We all have that bag of tricks that we keep when the universe isn't rational and our God is out of town. I think about that white, mangy rabbits foot that I paid a quarter for at the carnival in seventy-eight, from the gypsy woman hawking her magic. She claimed that I would obtain late night wishes of money, fame, and girls. How many actually happened? I gladly trusted her crooked smile and smudged mascara. I think about the cross I received for my First Holy Communion while attending St. Mary's of perpetual bad habits. I would chant at early Mass as did the old Polish women wrapped in their faith, all while holding their childhood rosaries. I prayed that my impure thoughts would be forgiven, while the shining cross hung outside my suit protecting me against teenage harlots and perverted priests. I think about the crystals from Arizona that were brought back by my great Aunt Margaret, who told me that they could have magical powers. I tried channeling Geronimo numerous times and did find the warrior in me, but like him, I faded into the distant hills and watched from a distance. I think about the holy water in a tiny bottle from the Vatican, that was blessed by Pope John Paul II. I should probably drink it and see what happens. Perhaps there is a shelf life of miracles in a bottle? I have at least made it half way. As time creeps by with mystery, I need to find a new bag of tricks that can help me see the next day.

Cardinal

There were three cardinal nestlings,
on the edge of the honeysuckle.

I nearly beheaded them like,
a medieval torturer with my hedge clippers.

Their parents choice of flora was not the best.
Turning reddish-gray with beaks agape, they looked
at me for food and protection.

We all are vulnerable to the dark shadows.
Sadly, either a feral cat or blacksnake knew
this all too well.

Seattle Peep Show

Dank Seattle night. Slanting hill in the market smells of the Pacific. The aged marque sign of yellowed bulbs hangs above the door advertising the flesh of the day. Union girls at twenty-five five bucks an hour dance for a quarter. Like pac-man, they wobble-wobble for a jukebox fantasy. They wave and smile, wiggle and worm and spin to the greatest hits. This ain't a seventies dance show. Black, yellow, white. Big ones, small ones, fit and fat. The booths are jammed with these ancient mariners and tired woodsmen from the Puget Sound who beg for spare change from strangers. Whiskey, cigarettes, and unkempt faces are supporting characters in this late night drama of the sexually charged. They all laugh like stoned monkeys getting caught by mother superior. Late night erections will end up in dark alley fights. A buffet between glass and stained curtains, keeps these animals away from the pretty meat.

Gaining Speed

Seeing her

he felt her

by the road

that had many

roads

which led to other roads

that he did not know

but he knew she would

take the road to leave

him,

in which

he decided to take

the road that simply

would welcome him back.

Zodiac

I am the shaggy, white mountain goat, climber of untouched skies. I wake before dawn and watch the sunrise hover and break the horizon. A morning frost breath can be seen, as the endless game trails look like harvest mazes, that can take you to the ageless mountain monk. What lies in front of me is snow, scree, granite, and towering canopies of biblical aged, bristlecone pines. I sense carnivorous predators lurking in the shadows ready to bounce and consume. I blend in with it all above the clouds, and stop, as there is nothing more to climb, but uncertainties. Can one turn on their own Zodiac sign? Shape shifting transformation from warm blooded to cold.
I am the spring fed fish. I am the limestone swimmer who is jacked on slated, eastern drakes and spinning mayflies. I am surrounded by both alpine scenery and Rockwell inspired farm lands. I am the salmonid. I am the river monster without any arms. My colors will change in seasonal arrival, like a underwater chameleon. I will feel the eddies under my gills and find refuge where I can be left alone. I fear the birds of prey and the fishermen with their rods. Our lives are short like the food we eat, and how we mate. In time I will move upstream for that final push towards nirvana and a new beginning.

Grade School

Love was the pretty girl who walked to school with him. Love actually was a pool flesh mixed with sugar and everything in between. He waited with his Batman lunchbox for her at the corner each day, with fresh daisies in his hand. He had picked them from the divorcee's front lawn, since he gave her free newspapers from time to time. Love would smell the yellowed little creatures as she twisted her hair, and placed the daisies in her math book. Sometimes she would thank him, and sometimes she would laugh wildly as the wind, and toss the flowers in the air. He would watch them fall from her delicate little hands onto the pavement, and eventually find them floating in the nearby river, where he would swim. He imagined they would make it to the oceans, where he had never been. The river was filled with this young man's haunted afterthoughts. The rocks of these waters hide his letters of proposals and youthful memories too. History was no longer when he went his way, but the waters never changed for him. He reminded himself that slanting rivers will always part and never look back.

Fish Fry

Blue-haired ladies in black laced hair nets, that could cover the Sea of Galilee, are moving fish faster than the apostles twelve this Friday afternoon during Lent. From battered bowl to deep fryer in repetition, the cod fillets are soon golden. The smell of hot oil and hair spray is a poison cocktail that the good book never mentioned. Saints and sinners marvel at their ten dollar dinners. Fried fish with fries, potato cakes, cole slaw, or pierogies are the choices. The church of redeemers is feeding the hungry. Old men with bellies and wrinkled hands sit in corners like old mobsters, talking loudly and tapping their canes on the wood covered floors. Mothers feed their children in small corner tables with plastic forks. Different faces from different races appear at the door with money in hand. The deep fryers continue to sizzle and the dirty dishes pile next to the old women in white aprons. There is chatter, polka music, and the underlying sense of a movable, communal feast.

Early Morning

Can a decade pass so swiftly that I don't remember how these babies became little people? They speak in articulate sentences and want things other than food. They loathe me when proper behavior is required. When did this all occur? They remain silent, like sleeping bears this morning during hibernation. I make the rounds like a seasoned corrections officer ready to call it quits, but needs a few more years to collect his pension. I look into the mirror and introduce myself this morning as I don't recognize this man. My voice sounds familiar and my nudity isn't so shocking to me.
Not bad I say to myself, as I flex to see what can move at this hour. Before the sun rises, the normality of the neighborhood remains a constant; red bricked homes, manicured lawns of green grass, and sun coming through the blinds creating shadow monsters that will soon wake the beloved. A stillness before we clock into the world. Those brief moments when we think that a huge secret may be revealed by the great horned owl that remains deep into the woods of our sub-consciousness. Only the echoing of hoot-hoot-hoot, is a welcoming sign. The day must begin.

Spring Flowers

I took the children to the cemetery
where they played among the etched
names of granite.

The sun created long
shadows in the distance, as I took a
walk to my father's grave.

Voices of the young never sounded
so beautiful. They did not know him
like I did, nor did they have a chance
to call him grandfather.

This place is still strange to me,
but yet the souls welcomed me without
judgment.

I see the widow has
planted her spring flowers again.
This gives her peace.

October On A Hillside Along The Dunraven Pass

I can see you as you creep against my skin. Moon glow.
Your creamy presence is pushing the day behind once
again, giving the sun a few more minutes to finish its
work. Your boldness and impending message of what is
to come, is very clear and near. The high country grizzlies,
who have been clawing for grubs the last six hours, don't
care about a calender. The audience has arrived, much
like the circus, including myself. The whitebark pines stand
straight in tight formation carpeting the valley below with
a greenish shag. Their canopy of countless acres has burnt
to the ground, reappeared, and will burn again. Cinnamon
girl and her adolescent cub bend up and down, then disappear,
amusing the long lens bipedalers who wait for action. Bears
have done this far beyond six thousand years, and haven't had
time to ponder it otherwise. I am lucky enough to bear this
witness.

Brains

How can I watch the debate
when their party has let the
zombies into their house?
The endless devouring of brains
is making me hungry. What
will be left of this country when
the "new" right is so wrong?
I shall drink a bottle of
tempranillo and gorge on fancy
salami and the best manchego
cheese I can find. When they
are done in Washington, they
may come look for me. I will
be waiting for them with my
critical thinking skills and leftist
book of poetry.

Birth

The lines were shaped at forty-five degree angles. White lies, I told myself a pitch between the pines on the endless face. I recognized this place from a dream. A white bear standing sniffing downwind. He catches a glimpse of me as I break trail. His ears twitch, listening to the wind that makes branches communicate with each other. My slight movements trigger his disappearance into the forest. Gone is the blur of blackness against the empty canvas of winter. I am reawakened by this bear ghost. The season has chosen me as its own. It makes no judgement of my flaws, as I continue to inhale only in-between the passing of flakes that seem to coat my throat. When there is light above me, I look for answers that dangle from the sky. A hanging thread of interjection seems plausible. I sigh as my age tells me to reason and turn back. I want to know what lays beyond what I can't see. Breaking through the shards of granite, I continue to push through the endless white. Its grasp, holding me steady, not promising me anything in return. I hear laughter coming from the anthropomorphic clouds and accept this proposition of the absurd. Snow drifts as a pinwheel of life rolls along this alpine highway.

Poor Kids

They get to wear the leftover clothing from
St. Vincent De Paul while they see the glitter
of newness on others, on their first day of school.
Trickle down poverty is popular. Study hard
and you won't need free lunches they are told.
The populist right wingers bark, while slashing
another program. They move around from
home to home, never feeling secure. Fast food
fills the already emptiness inside. A free toy
does wonders. Often they don't have a choice.
They hope that Santa brings them something
nice, but it's usually a sweater to grow into
or nothing at all. They understand their own
poverty, when they don't get invited, or have
parties of their own. I see them in stores
wandering the aisles, always wanting but never
getting. The one-percent will always look down
at these children. They need to have big
imaginations to set themselves free. We all know
some child like this. Often they grow into adult
ghosts who never smile, all wanting to be reborn
and to have another childhood.

Clarity

Against the back light of the Sawtooths, I walk alone
in between the yellow breezy aspens and river cottonwoods.
Dusk. Matted hues of plein air strokes, are represented
here. A canvas filled with playful pastels. I seek one more
cast that will cut through the dryness of the day and wetness
of the river, and heighten my mortal senses. Forgetting who
I am almost instantly excites me. With attempted grace, the
rhythm of arm and rod, line and fly, I will accept this addiction.
Sweeping lines shoot across open water with a yellow sally.
Working the surface mesmerizes and eludes me at the same
time. Repeat again and again. Hemingway's masculine prose
of these waters finally brought me here; yet these waters
show me androgyny. Powerful. Graceful. Illusionary. I am
beneath the world that has placed me tying that soon to be
last fly against the darkening sky. Even in black, there is clarity.
I am no longer filled with disillusionment, as the river has finally
called me back.

Easter Beard

The candles light the altar and burn like tiki torches, mesmerizing me as I sit in a near trance while entertaining my own history from inside these immigrant built walls of red brick. My genuflection is a reflection from past to present. What is it I feel? The boy has been long gone. I have created this new face. But when did this happen? Spring meant getting ready for baseball, cutting grass, trout fishing, and trying to get through the Easter season. I really tried my best at forty days, but often failed even though there were plenty of hanging crosses to remind me of my commitment. I was named after a saint and my father, who I later canonized myself, when I finally understood his life. The burning incense clouds the air, like it did thirty five years before. I couldn't take it then and I can't take it now. I can still see the girls dressed in white who never prayed louder than me. They sat in rows with their small hands pressed together with fingers pointing to the heavens above. I really didn't want them to know what I prayed for when I was their age. At twelve, they were the angels in the outfield who I would dream about, while the others chanted in Latin and prayed the rosary over and over. The organist, who bounced notes off of the high ceilings creating holy madness, is the same, only now he uses a cane to the second floor. Those wingless beings have gone away. Those girls now have birthed their own, and I am here again stroking the greys out of my Easter beard, and staring at the stained glass windows that show pain and suffering. I no longer ask for anything as I use the kneeler out of childhood habit. The music starts, and I don't know the words anymore as the children sing softly against my silence.

Searching For A Muse

I went to the edge of time and I was blood thirsty.
I listened to a song that I could not hear. I read a book
that had blank pages. I drank from the stream but it was
dry. I kissed a girl and her mouth disappeared. I looked
into the early night sky, and the clouds swallowed the stars.
I reached towards the fading sun, and it started to melt.
I finally put my hands deep into the soil and found something
that poured imagination back into my veins. I was able to
breathe. The muse was not from this planet.

In The Name Of The Father

Deep river,
shady cottonwood grove,
slurping brownie puckers up.

Spring air, hallowed water divine,
river sirens rise, setting sun will set
me free from any evil.

River otter swims close to me and
disappears towards the willows
and bank side home.

A drop of mountain water,
I am my mothers child, father made
her cavernous moist my home,
under the sweetness of her fluid.

I am but a water child returning to church,
heading deeper into the abyss and satisfying
my mortal shortcomings.

Hop Yard Harvest (Ode to the Owl Farm)

One hundred and twenty days. It's late August and the vines have spoken. The petaled cones of green with aromas of pine, grapefruit, and zesty citrus hang so delicately like ancient Christmas ornaments above the wet grass and clay soil. Heat, moist with Mason-Dixon Line humidity, imbues the late afternoon air. I dream of a dank India pale ale or an easy drinking session ale. I look at all the rows and wonder where we should all begin. Like old farmhands we start with one, two, and then three cones at a time. The leaves are smooth, curved, and without sharp thorns. The bees buzz nearby in a frenzy. An orb spider comes out and takes a peek. The beetles that had been the culprits of trying to destroy the crops, fly away in distress. Intoxicated by these tiny cones, the picking goes on into early evening after three straight days. We sweat as our cotton shirts can no longer hold the mixture of summer work. We bend. We cut. We haul. The bandanas of blue and red keep our eyes dry from the constant slow drips. The cones are piled high into the truck ready to take to the next process of drying. The depleted vines now naked and wrapped like used up garden hoses, are no longer mighty green giants. The naked poles will remain until the flollowing spring. Cascade, Zeus, Centennial, and Nugget hops. Aromatic visions that will send me in search for a cold one to drink, as the days work on the farm is over.

Streaming Transcendence

Glass water, polarized eyes of copper. The sun steeps in color of apocalyptic blood orange where the currents of tiny beings from sky and water come together for an early evening of show and tell. Numerous brown winged, black bodies move from top to bottom. From water we all emerge. Clustering the surface, these aquatic macro-invertebrates begin their ritual of the finality of their abbreviated existence. There is no real time here. A rave without music and ecstasy. Madness on the river. Fluid bodies bend like invisible light rays. Tiny sips become giant gulps from brown, speckled giants. This is the way it has always been. Clouds move and light blends in old Kodachrome, as the greens of river riparian vegetation lay heavy along the paths that zig and zag. Fleshy missiles rise from the abyss. Continuous flow from a single motherly drop fills these banks that empty a thousand miles from here. The legless, frenzied are violently cold blooded. Again and again. There is no right or wrong. Both personalities from sky and water duel to the end. The overtures of life and death are symphonic to my senses that never seem to dull. When it is over, there is only the sound of the osprey that descends from the cottonwoods above. My existence predates nothing here, as I am simply a voyeur witnessing the all too obvious.

www.ingramcontent.com/pod-product-compliance
Lightning Source LLC
Chambersburg PA
CBHW032058040426
42449CB00007B/1124